The Sinn Fein Reb

I Saw It.

Mrs. Hamilton Norway

Alpha Editions

This edition published in 2023

ISBN : 9789357933230

Design and Setting By
Alpha Editions
www.alphaedis.com
Email - info@alphaedis.com

The Sinn Fein Rebellion as I Saw It

Royal Hibernian Hotel,

Dawson Street, Dublin,

Tuesday, April 25th.

DEAREST G.,—I am afraid by this time you will have seen a good deal in the papers to cause you alarm, and as it is impossible to get a letter or telegram through, I will write you a detailed account of what we are going through and post it to you at the first opportunity.

To begin at the beginning, the Sinn Fein movement, which is now frankly revolutionary and which must not be confounded with Redmond's Nationalist Party, has been in existence for years, but has always been looked on as a small body of cranks who were thirsting for notoriety. Redmond's policy has always been to treat them with utter contempt, and the Government adopted his view.

Since the outbreak of war this movement, encouraged no doubt by German intrigue and German money, has grown by leaps and bounds, and about eighteen months ago a large number broke away from Redmond's National Volunteers and formed a volunteer force which they called the Irish Volunteers. They are frankly and openly revolutionary, and when it became known some months ago that they were obtaining large quantities of arms and ammunition various persons did all they could to open the eyes of the authorities to the dangerous situation that was growing up. But as the explanation was always given that the force was for national defence only, the Government failed to take any steps to put down the movement.

During the past six months the body has grown enormously, as many as seven hundred recruits being enlisted on one night, and of course doing enormous harm to recruiting for the Army. On St. Patrick's Day they held a large review of several battalions, armed, and the trams were all held up for about an hour in College Green. Up to the last moment there was hope that this would be stopped, but protests were like a voice crying in the wilderness. Another time they held a full dress rehearsal of what has actually taken place when they "took" the Castle, St. Stephen's Green, and various buildings. About a month ago one of their meetings in the country was broken up and the two leaders arrested and deported to England. A huge meeting of protest was held at the Mansion House, almost opposite this hotel, and attended by the Volunteers, all armed, who marched in procession. After the meeting they marched down Grafton Street, singing "Die Wacht am Rhein" and revolutionary songs; a slight disturbance with the police took place and some shots were fired. People began to ask anxiously what next? but the Government looked on and smiled and H. tore his hair.

On Saturday we were going to tea with friends at Bray, when just as we were starting H. got an "official" from the Castle, so I went alone and he went to the Castle. News had come that a boat had been taken off the Kerry coast, landing ammunition, and a very important arrest had been made. Easter Sunday passed off in absolute calm, and yesterday (Easter Monday) morning H. said he had a lot of letters to write and he would go and write them at his club, almost next door to the Sackville Street G.P.O. He found he wanted to answer some letters that were in his desk at the G.P.O., so he walked over to his room and was just sitting down when his 'phone went, an urgent message to go at once to the Castle.

He had only just arrived there, and was in consultation with Sir M. N., when suddenly a volley of shots rang out at the Castle gate, and it was found armed bodies of men were in possession of the City Hall and other houses that commanded the other gates to the Castle, and anyone attempting to leave the Castle was shot. All the officials in the Castle were prisoners.

News quickly came that the magazine in the Park had been taken, the G.P.O., two stations, and all the houses that commanded O'Connell Bridge had been stormed and taken, and the rebels had taken St. Stephen's Green, where they were entrenching themselves.

Meantime, knowing nothing of this, N. went for a country motor bike ride, and I did some sewing and wrote letters, etc., and when N. came in about 12.30 I said I wanted a walk before lunch and we would walk down to the club and meet H. The streets were quiet and deserted till we crossed O'Connell Bridge, when N. remarked there was a dense crowd round Nelson's Pillar, but we supposed it was a bank holiday crowd waiting for trams. We were close to the General Post Office when two or three shots were fired, followed by a volley, and the crowd began rushing down towards the bridge, the people calling out "Go back, go back; the Sinn Feiners are firing." N. said, "You'd better go back, Mother; there's going to be a row; I'll go on to the club and find Dad"; so I turned and fled with the crowd and got back safely to the hotel.

Here was excitement and consternation. Every moment people were coming in with tales of civilians being shot in the streets, and houses commanding wide thoroughfares and prominent positions being taken possession of by the Sinn Feiners, whose method was to go in detachments of four or six armed men, ring the bell, and demand to see the owners of the houses. In many instances they were away for the Easter holidays, when the frightened servants were just turned into the street to go where they would; but if the master or mistress were at home they were told with a revolver at their heads that the house was required by the Irish Republic for strategic purposes, and the owners were given the option of leaving the house or remaining as prisoners in the basement. A few elected to do this in preference to leaving all their household goods to the mercy of the rebels; but most thought "discretion the better part of valour" and cleared out to friends, in some instances only to be hunted out from their house of refuge a second time. The windows of the houses were then barricaded with a reckless disregard to valuable furniture, which in many cases was turned into the street to form barricades.

You remember my nice housemaid Mary, gentle as a dove and timid as a hare. I had got her a very nice place with a lady who had taken a large house in Leeson Street close to the bridge and commanding Fitzwilliam Place. She went this morning by appointment to meet the lady at the house and found the Sinn Feiners on the steps, who pointed their revolvers at her and told her to clear out. She was so scared she nearly fell into the area, and came to the hotel looking like a ghost.

But to return to our own adventures. Directly I got back to the hotel I rang up the club and was told by old MacDermott, the hall-porter, that H. had left the club at 11.30 to go to the G.P.O.,[9] saying he would be back shortly; but he had not returned, and since then the Post Office had been stormed and the guard shot or overpowered, and the Sinn Feiners were in possession of the whole building, and firing volleys on the police from the windows! Imagine my feelings!

About 1.30 N. returned, having failed to find any trace of H., but he had seen some cavalry shot coming out of Talbot Street into Sackville Street. The first three or four were just picked off their horses and fell wounded or dead, and the horses were shot. He said the scene of excitement in Sackville Street was indescribable. We were just going in to lunch when a telephone message came through saying H. was at the Castle but could not leave.

This relieved our minds as to his fate, and after lunch I was kept busy at the telephone answering distracted messages from Post Office officials who were wandering about looking for H. At about 4 p.m. N. returned from a tour of inspection, and told me all was quiet in Sackville Street, and begged me to go out with him and see the G.P.O.

I quaked rather, but we set off and reached Sackville Street safely.

Over the fine building of the G.P.O. floated a great green flag with the words "Irish Republic" on it in large white letters. Every window on the ground floor was smashed and barricaded with furniture, and a big placard announced "The Headquarters of the Provisional Government of the Irish Republic." At every window were two men with rifles, and on the roof the parapet was lined with men. H.'s room appeared not to have been touched, and there were no men at his windows.

We stood opposite and were gazing, when suddenly two shots were fired, and, seeing there was likely to be an ugly rush, I fled again, exhorting N. to take refuge at the club.

He never reached the club, but came back to the hotel, and we had tea, and he then went to inspect St. Stephen's Green.

He found all round the Green, just inside the railings among the shrubberies, the rebels had dug deep pits or holes, and in every hole were three men. They had barricaded the street opposite the Shelbourne Hotel, and there had been a lot of firing and several people killed, and shots had gone into the hotel, which is, as you know, a fine building facing the Green.

All the evening we heard firing in all directions of the city and rumours of troops having arrived from the Curragh. While at dinner another message came through from H. to say we were not to be alarmed; he was quite safe, but might not get home that night.

After dinner N. went out to see if he could get near the Castle, but he found awful fighting. The troops were storming the City Hall and using machine-guns, and it was too "unhealthy" for him to get near, so he came back at 9 and went to bed.

I stayed up in case of being wanted on the 'phone, and at 11.30 p.m. went up to my room, and a few minutes later H. walked in, to my immense relief.

The troops had arrived from the Curragh at about 5 p.m. and had promptly stormed the City Hall, which commanded the main gate of the Castle, and had taken it after fierce fighting.

H. saw prisoners being brought into the Castle yard, and when all was quiet he and several other officials crept out and reached their various homes.

People are appalled at the utter unpreparedness of the Government. In the face of a huge body of trained and armed men, openly revolutionary, they had taken no precautions whatever for the defence of the city in the event of an outbreak. At the beginning of the war H. obtained a military guard, armed, for the G.P.O., and they have always been there. When the outbreak occurred yesterday the armed guard were there, but with no ammunition! The sergeant was wounded in two places and the rest overpowered.

All night the firing continued. Between 1 and 2 a.m. it was awful, and I lay and quaked. It was all in the direction of the Castle.

This morning we hear the military are pouring into the city, and are in the Shelbourne Hotel and Trinity College.

The rebels have barricaded Sackville Street, and it is expected to be very fierce fighting over the G.P.O. It is terrible!

All our valuables were stored in H.'s safe and cupboard when we gave up our house, and all our dear F.'s books, sword, and all his possessions, which we value more than anything else in the world. We would not trust them with the stored furniture.

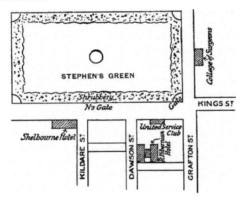

Yesterday afternoon the mob broke all the windows in various streets and looted all the shops. The streets were strewn with clothes, boots, furniture, tram cushions, and everything you can imagine.

While I am writing now there is incessant firing in St. Stephen's Green, and we fear there may be street fighting in this street.

In case you have forgotten, I will put a little plan here (see p. 14).

Tuesday, 5 p.m.

This morning martial law was proclaimed (I will try and get a copy of the proclamation) at 11.30 and the rebels given four hours to surrender.

A cruiser and two transports are said to have arrived at Kingstown, with troops from England. At 3.30 p.m., as there had been no surrender, the troops started to clear St. Stephen's Green, and raked it with machine-guns from the top of the Shelbourne Hotel and the United Service Club. We hear there are many casualties. N. has just come in, and says a big fire is raging in Sackville Street in the shops opposite the G.P.O., supposed to have been caused by the mob finding fireworks in a toy shop. The fire brigade arrived almost at once and could easily have overcome the fire, but the brigade was fired on by the Sinn Feiners, making it impossible for them to bring the engines into action, and they had to beat a retreat and leave the shops to burn themselves out. N. says the troops are clearing the houses of rebels behind Dame Street and the region of the Castle, and there is a lot of firing. It has turned to rain, which has cleared the streets of people.

A telegram has just come from the Admiralty stopping the mail boat from crossing. No boat has gone to-day, and we are absolutely cut off.

All the roads leading out of Dublin are in the hands of the rebels.

H. and N. have just come in, having seen Dr. W. (now Major W.), Surgeon to the Forces in Ireland. He told them that so far we had had about 500 casualties, two-thirds of them being civilians, shot in the streets.

The first thing Dr. W. heard of the outbreak was a 'phone message telling him to go at once to the Shelbourne as a man had been shot. He supposed it was a case of suicide, so jumped into his car and went off, fortunately in mufti. In Nassau Street his car was stopped and he was ordered to get out by rebels. He attempted to argue, and was told if he did not obey instantly he would be shot. Had he been in uniform he would have been shot at sight. As a civilian doctor they allowed him to go, and he took his bag and ran. He found three men shot in the Shelbourne, and a boy was shot as he reached the door.

Wednesday, April 26th, 9.30 a.m.

Last evening was quiet till we went to bed at 10.30, when almost immediately a furious machine-gun fire began. It seemed just at the back of the hotel, but was really at the top of Grafton Street and the street leading to Mercer's Hospital. It lasted about twenty minutes, and then almost immediately after we got into bed a 'phone came that H. was to go at once to the Vice-Regal Lodge in the Phœnix Park, so he dressed and tried every way to get a motor; but of course no motor would go out. After some delay he got the field ambulance of the fire brigade at Dr. W.'s suggestion; but when it came the men told H. they had been carrying wounded all day, and that they had been constantly stopped by pickets and the car searched, and if they went and the car was stopped and found to contain H. they would undoubtedly all be shot; so H. considered it too risky, and it had to be abandoned. Eventually his Excellency gave his instructions over the 'phone, first in French, but that particular 'phone either did not speak or did not understand French, so eventually he took the risk of the 'phone being tapped and gave them in English. At last H. got to bed about 1 a.m., to be at the 'phone again at 5 a.m.

While we were dressing a terrific bombardment with field guns began— the first we had heard—and gave me cold shivers. The sound seemed to come from the direction of the G.P.O., and we concluded they were bombarding it. It went on for a quarter of an hour—awful! big guns and machine-guns—and then ceased, but we hear they were bombarding Liberty Hall, the headquarters of Larkin and the strikers two years ago, and always a nest of sedition. It is now crammed with Sinn Feiners. The guns were on H.M.S. *Helga*, that came up the river and smashed it from within about three hundred yards. It made me feel quite sick.

We think that they are leaving the Post Office for a time with the hope that when other strongholds are taken the Republican Government will surrender. H. has just been summoned to the Castle, and there is no knowing when he will be back. All who go out carry their lives in their hands. I went out twice yesterday, but we were turned back by shots being fired from upper windows, and the Lord Lieutenant has issued a proclamation begging people to keep in their houses, so I must restrain my curiosity.

All the shops remain closed, and no papers are issued except the proclamation, and we know nothing of what is going on in other parts of Ireland. But there are wild rumours of insurrection in Cork and other places.

This morning there is firing again in St. Stephen's Green, so the rebels are still there.

N. did a very fine thing yesterday. After the Green had been raked by our machine-gun fire he strolled up, in his casual way, to see the result! In front of one of the side gates in the railings, which are seven feet high and spiked three ways, he saw a small group of men peering into the Green. He went to see what they were looking at. The rebels had barricaded the gate, which opened inwards, by putting one of the heavy garden seats against it *upside down* and on the top of it another *right side up*, and lying full length on the seat, face downwards, was a man, a civilian, with all his lower jaw blown away and bleeding profusely. N. immediately climbed the railings and dropped down on the Sinn Fein side and found that the man was still living; he then turned and fairly cursed the men who were looking on, and asked if there was not one man enough to come over the railings and help him. Whereupon three men climbed over and together they lifted down the seat with the poor creature on it, dragged away the other seat, when they were able to open the gate, and then brought out the seat and the man on it and carried him to the nearest hospital, where he died in about five minutes.

N.'s theory is he was probably one of the civilians taken prisoner by the Sinn Fein the previous day, and was trying to escape from the awful machine-gun fire when he was shot down and fell back on to the seat. It was a terrible case.

The rebels from St. Stephen's Green are now also in possession of the College of Surgeons and are firing across the Green at the troops in the Shelbourne Hotel.

Lord S. tells me that 30,000 troops were landed at Kingstown this morning, and we hear they are amazed at their reception, as they had been told that they were going to quell a rebellion in Ireland, and lo! on their arrival at Kingstown the whole population turned out to cheer them, giving them food, cigarettes, chocolate, and everything the hospitable inhabitants could provide, so that the puzzled troops asked plaintively: "Who then are we going to fight, and where is the rebellion?" However, they were quickly disillusioned, for in marching into Dublin, when they reached Ballsbridge they came within range of several houses occupied by Sinn Feiners, and without a word of warning the battalion of Sherwood Foresters came under terrible cross-fire and were just shot down, unable to return a single shot. I have not heard how many casualties occurred, but two or three officers and many men were killed and a number wounded. So surely soon we must be relieved.

Thursday, April 27th.

Last night the mail boat left carrying passengers, and if it goes this evening Lord S. may be crossing, and he will take this to you.

Yesterday afternoon and evening there was terrible fighting. The rebels hold all the bridges over the canal, one on the tram line between this and Blackrock, another at the end of Baggot Street, and the other at Leeson Street. The fighting was terrible, but in the end we took the Leeson Street bridge, and I hope still hold it, as this opens a road to Kingstown. We failed to take the other two.

At the end of Lower Mount Street the rebels held the schools, and there was fierce fighting: our troops failed to surround the schools, and in the end, when they at last took them by a frontal attack with the loss of eighteen men and one officer, only one rebel was taken, the rest having escaped by the back.

Yesterday, to our great indignation, the public-houses were allowed to be open from 2 till 5, though every shop, bank, and public building was closed—just to inflame the mob, it could not have been on any other grounds; and yet at 8 p.m., after being on duty from 5 a.m., H. could not get a whiskey and soda, or even a glass of cider with his dinner, as it was out of hours. I was *furious*!

I must close this, as Lord S. has come in and says he expects to go to-night and will take this and H.'s report, so I will start a fresh letter to-morrow.

Don't worry overmuch about us. We quite expect to come out of this, but if we don't N. is *yours*.

L. N.

Second Letter.

Dearest G.,—After all my letter did not get off last night, as the roads were too dangerous to admit of Dr. W. motoring Lord S. to Kingstown. He got a permit to pass our troops, but there were too many Sinn Fein positions and snipers to make it possible for them to pass through.

If the position improves, he will go to-night, so I may be able to send this too, if I can write enough to make it worth while, but I am still rather shaky from a fright I had last night.

Yesterday morning the Red Cross ambulance sent in to the hotel to ask for volunteer workers to act as stretcher-bearers and do all sorts of jobs connected with the Red Cross, and N. and several men staying in the hotel volunteered. I was glad he should, as he is of course safer attached to the Red Cross than roaming the streets making rescues on his own, and if he was killed or wounded we should at least hear of it. But the risks are many and great, as in this kind of street fighting, where all the firing is from windows or from housetops, the ambulance are frequently under fire.

However, N. having volunteered promptly went off, and we saw him no more. While we were having dinner Mr. O'B., who had been out all day with the ambulance, was dining with us. H. was called to the telephone to receive this message: "You must not expect to see or hear from me till this is over."

H. asked who the message was from, and the answer came back: "Your son" in a voice that H. was sure was not N.'s. H. then asked where the message came from, and was told "The Castle."

He returned to us greatly perturbed, and we held a consultation. We all agreed there was only one interpretation to be put on it, viz., that N. had been taken prisoner by the rebels, and that someone who was well disposed to H. had taken this opportunity of letting him know, and that saying the message came from the Castle was just a blind. H. rang up the head of the Red Cross, and he told us only two of the Red Cross volunteers were missing who had been out that day, and both of them were known, and N. was not one of them, so we were still more mystified.

It then occurred to H. that it might be possible to trace back the message and find out where it really had been sent from, so he called up the exchange, and after a little delay he heard the message had actually been sent from the Castle and by N., who was there.

Imagine our relief! though still completely in the dark as to why the boy had not come back like other workers, and why we were not to expect to see him again.

Next morning in walked the truant, not best pleased that we had been inquiring for him. His explanation was quite simple. He had been attached to a branch of the ambulance that had its depôt at the Castle, so worked from there and returned to the Castle at night. Hearing this, and not knowing in the least to what part of the city his work would take him, and the impossibility of sending any message or note to tell us where he was, and knowing how anxious I should be if he did not return, he asked the Castle authorities if he might send a message to *relieve our minds*! He was told he might do so, but it must only be one sentence, and he must have the censor in the box with him. This so flustered N. that he could think of nothing to say but the words I have quoted; they seemed to him to express the position exactly, and he never dreamt of the interpretation we should put on them. As it was I spent an hour I don't ever like to remember and which unnerved me more than I thought possible, and all I got was a trouncing from N. for being so "nervy." Surely much is expected from mothers these days!

The volunteer workers, among other things, enter houses where there are known to be wounded Sinn Feiners and bring them out and take them to hospitals.

This N. was doing yesterday. One of the most awful things in this terrible time is that there must be scores of dead and dying Sinn Feiners, many of them mere lads, that no one can get at in the houses, and where they will remain till after the rebellion; and in some cases the houses take fire and they are all burnt. However, whatever is possible is being done.

Yesterday was the worst day we have had, as there was desperate fighting in Grafton Street, just at our back, and the side streets; and several volleys in our street.

In the morning I was sitting on a settee near the window of the lounge, knitting and looking out and listening to the firing in Grafton Street, when shots were fired just outside our windows, and Mr. B., the manager, came in and said, "We must shut all the shutters, Mrs. N., it is getting a bit too hot, and I am taking no risks." So all the shutters were closed, and I moved to the drawing-room above, which also overlooks the street.

All the afternoon an awful battle raged in the neighbourhood of the river and quays, and the din of the great guns and machine-guns was tremendous. We now have 30,000 troops and plenty of artillery and machine-guns, so the result cannot be uncertain, though there is desperate work to be done before the end is in sight.

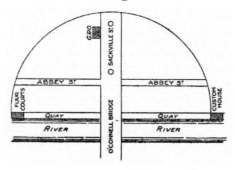

The troops are said to have formed a huge semi-circle with the G.P.O. as the centre, and, starting from the river, are driving the rebels back street by street, till eventually they will be in a small enclosure, when they will bombard it to pieces.

The G.P.O. has such valuable records, etc., and the contents of the safes are so precious, that they will not raze it to the ground if they can help it; but it has so much subterranean space, that would afford cover to thousands of Sinn Feiners, that we hear they are going to fire some "gas" shells into it and then rush it!

Up to yesterday afternoon they had got to Abbey Street on the right, and no doubt were closing in equally on other sides. The shells had started several fires; nearly all the shops on the quay on the side of the Custom House were burning yesterday afternoon, and later in the evening many others broke out.

I cannot give you any idea of what it was like when I went to bed. I sent for Mrs. B., the manager's wife, such a splendid little woman, and together we watched it from my window, which is high up and looked in the right direction.

It was the most awe-inspiring sight I have ever seen. It seemed as if the whole city was on fire, the glow extending right across the heavens, and the red glare hundreds of feet high, while above the roar of the fires the whole air seemed vibrating with the noise of the great guns and machine-guns. It was an inferno! We remained spell-bound, and I can't tell you how I longed for you to see it. We had only just come down from the window—we had been standing on the window ledge leaning out—when H. came and told us no one was to look out of the windows as there was cross-firing from the United Service Club and another building, and Mr. O'B., who was watching the fires from his window, had a bullet a few inches from his head!!

About 2 a.m. I woke to find the room illuminated in spite of dark blinds and curtains, and I rushed to the window and saw an enormous fire; it seemed to be in the direction of the Four Courts, which is in the hands of the Sinn Feiners, and we hear this morning that a portion of the buildings was burnt last night.[A]

[A] This was incorrect; it was the Linen Hall barracks that were burnt.

Yesterday Lord S. had a narrow escape from a sniper who has been worrying this street for two days and could not be located. He was picking off soldiers during the fighting in Grafton Street, but later turned his attention to the cross streets between this and Grafton Street, and there as nearly as possible got Lord S., who was coming back to us from the Castle.

The military thought the man was on *our* roof, which made us all bristle with indignation—the mere idea of the wretch being on our hotel; but a thorough search proved he was not here, though he evidently had access to *some* roof.

In this respect we are much better off than our friends the V.'s. They came into their town house only about a month ago, and being in Upper Mount Street it was in one of the most active haunts of the snipers. They had several on their roof, and when they went up to bed at night they could hear the snipers walking about and talking on the roof. Does it not make one creep to think of it? Mr. V. had his bed put on the upper landing exactly under the trap-door on to the roof, so that had the rebels attempted to enter the house at night they would have come down "plop" on to him in his bed. He surrounded himself with all the arms he could muster, and the wretched Mrs. V. lay in bed and quaked, expecting any minute to hear a battle royal raging outside her bedroom door. In this street an old lady of seventy-three was shot through the leg in her own room, and was taken to Dr. W.'s home, where she had to have her leg amputated; and in another house a servant flashed on her electric light when going to bed and was instantly shot through the head! Our friend Miss K. also had a narrow escape. She had only just left her drawing-room, when a bullet passed straight through the room and buried itself in a picture.

Yesterday afternoon, when the firing in Grafton Street was over, the mob appeared and looted the shops, clearing the great provision shops and others. From the back of this hotel you look down on an alley that connects with Grafton Street,—and at the corner, the shop front in Grafton Street, but with a side entrance into this lane, is a very large and high-class fruiterer. From the windows we watched the proceedings, and I never saw anything so brazen! The mob were chiefly women and children, with a sprinkling of men. They swarmed in and out of the side door bearing huge consignments of bananas, the great bunches on the stalk, to which the children attached a cord and ran away dragging it along. Other boys had big orange boxes which they filled with tinned and bottled fruits. Women with their skirts held up received showers of apples and oranges and all kinds of fruit which were thrown from the upper windows by their pals; and ankle-deep on the ground lay all the pink and white and silver paper and paper shavings used for packing choice fruits. It was an amazing sight, and nothing daunted these people. Higher up at another shop we were told a woman was hanging out of a window dropping down loot to a friend, when she was shot through the head by a sniper, probably our man; the body dropped into the street and the mob cleared. In a few minutes a hand-cart appeared and gathered up the body, and instantly all the mob swarmed back to continue the joyful proceedings!

H. and Lord S. were sitting at the window for a few minutes yesterday when the fruit shop was being looted, and saw one of the funniest sights they had ever seen. A very fat, very blousy old woman emerged from the side street and staggered on to the pavement laden with far more loot than she could carry. In her arms she had an orange box full of fruit, and under her shawl she had a great bundle tied up which kept slipping down. Having reached the pavement, she put down her box and sat on it, and from her bundle rolled forth many tins of fruit. These she surveyed ruefully, calling on the Almighty and all the saints to help her!! From these she solemnly made her selection, which she bound up in her bundle and hoisted, with many groans and lamentations, on her back and made off with, casting back many longing looks at the pile of things left on the pavement, which were speedily disposed of by small boys.

On Wednesday when the looting was going on in Sackville Street a fine, large boot shop was receiving attention from swarms of looters. Ragged women and children were seen calmly sitting in the window trying on boots and shoes, and one old woman with an eye to future needs made up a bundle of assorted sizes and tied them up in her apron. She had only reached the pavement, when she bethought her to leave her bundle in a corner and return for a further consignment which she tied up in her shawl. On returning to the street great was her rage and indignation on finding the original bundle had disappeared. Then were there sore lamentations and violent abuse of the police, who could not even "protect the property of a poor old woman."

In Sackville Street was a very large shop called Clery's; for some reason the looters were afraid to start on it, and old women passed up and down gazing longingly at fur coats and silken raiment and saying sorrowfully, "Isn't Clery's broke yet?" and "Isn't it a great shame that Clery's is not broke!" Humour and tragedy are so intermixed in this catastrophe. A very delicate elderly lady who is staying here said to me this morning, in answer to my inquiry as to how she had slept: "I could not sleep at all. When the guns ceased the *awful silence* made me so nervous!" I know exactly what she meant. When the roar of the guns ceases you can *feel* the silence.

4 p.m.

When I had got so far this morning I got an urgent message from the Red Cross asking me to make more armlets for the workers. With two other ladies I had been making them yesterday, so I collected my helpers and we worked till lunch, when another request came that we would make four large Red Cross flags, as they were going to try to bury some of the dead and needed the flags for the protection of the parties. We have just finished them, and are wondering what will be the next call. It is such a good thing I have my sewing-machine here.

On Wednesday evening Lord S. was at Mercer's Hospital with a doctor when eleven dead were brought in, and a priest brought in a rifle he had taken from a dead Sinn Feiner. It had an inscription in German and the name of the factory in Berlin, which Lord S. copied. It is believed that nearly all the arms and ammunition are of German make, and it is said that the cruiser that was sunk on Saturday was bringing heavy guns and forty officers, but I don't know if there is any truth in that. The opinion is very strong that the Sinn Feiners were led to believe that they would have great German reinforcements, and that all they had to do was to hold the troops here for a couple of days while the Germans landed a big force on the west coast of Ireland. We also hear that Sir R. Casement has been shot in London, but you probably know a great deal more about that than I do, as we see no papers and are completely cut off from all news.

On Wednesday three of the ringleaders were caught, and it is said they were shot immediately! It is also believed that Larkin was shot on the top of a house in St. Stephen's Green, but as the rebels still hold the house it has not been possible to identify him, but he is said to have been here on Monday.[B]

[B] This was incorrect; it appears Larkin was not in Dublin.

5 p.m.

Colonel C. has just come in, having been in the thick of it for forty-eight hours. He tells us the Post Office has been set on fire by the Sinn Feiners, who have left it. If this is true, and it probably is, I fear we have lost all our valuable possessions, including my diamond pendant, which was in my jewel-case in H.'s safe.

To-day about lunch-time a horrid machine-gun suddenly gave voice very near us. We thought it was in this street, but it may have been in Kildare

Street; also the sniper reappeared on the roofs, and this afternoon was opposite my bedroom window judging from the sound. I pulled down my blinds. A man might hide for weeks on the roofs of these houses among the chimney stacks and never be found as long as he had access to some house for food. When we were working in my room this afternoon he fired some shots that could not have been more than twenty yards away.

The serious problem of food is looming rather near, as nothing has come into the city since Saturday. Boland's bakery, an enormous building, is in the hands of the rebels, who have barricaded all the windows with sacks of flour, and it is said it will have to be blown up. There is not a chance of getting them out in any other way. The rebels also have Jacob's biscuit factory, where there are still huge stores of flour. Every prominent building and every strategic position was taken before the authorities at the Castle woke to the fact that there was a rebellion!

I was almost forgetting to tell you how splendidly one of H.'s men behaved when the G.P.O. was taken. When the rebels took possession they demanded the keys from the man who had them in charge. He quietly handed over the keys, having first abstracted the keys of H.'s room!

Imagine such self-possession at such a terrible moment.

A young man has come to stay in the hotel who saw the taking of the G.P.O. He was staying at the hotel exactly opposite the building and went into the G.P.O. to get some stamps. As he was leaving the office a detachment of about fifteen Irish Volunteers marched up and formed up in front of the great entrance. He looked at them with some curiosity, supposing they were going to hold a parade; two more detachments arrived, and immediately the word of command was given, and they rushed in through the door. Shots were fired inside the building, and, as the young man said, he "hooked it" back to the hotel, which was one of those burnt a few days later. The whole thing occupied only a few moments, as, being Bank Holiday, there was only a small staff in the building.

6.30 p.m. A party of soldiers and a young officer have just arrived to search the roof for the sniper. They say he is on the roof of the annexe, which is connected with the main building by covered-in bridges. They are now on the roof and shots are being fired, so I expect they have spotted him.

When N. was out last night another ambulance had a bad experience. They had fetched three wounded Sinn Feiners out of a house, and were taking them to hospital, when they came under heavy fire. The driver was killed, so the man beside him took the wheel and was promptly wounded in both legs. The car then ran away and wrecked itself on a lamp post.

Another ambulance had to run the gauntlet and go to the rescue! On the whole as far as possible the rebels have respected the Red Cross, but not the white flag. In house-to-house fighting there can be no connected action, and yesterday when a house was being stormed the rebels hung out a white flag, and when the troops advanced to take them prisoners they were shot down from a house a few doors higher up the street, so now no more white flag signals are to be recognised. If they want to surrender they must come out and take their own risks.

We asked N. if he knew what had happened to the ambulance that had two men missing yesterday, and he told us they were in the act of entering a Sinn Fein house to bring out wounded with two other men when the ambulance came under such heavy fire that, as it contained one or two other wounded men, it had to beat a retreat and moved off. Two of the volunteer helpers ran after it and succeeded in reaching it and climbed in, but the other two took refuge in the area, and N. did not know how or when they were rescued. This is an instance of the extreme danger that attends the ambulance work. The marvel is that the casualties are so few.

Guinness's Brewery have made three splendid armoured cars by putting great long boilers six feet in diameter on to their large motor lorries. Holes are bored down the sides to let in air, and they are painted grey. The driver sits inside too. They each carry twenty-two men or a ton of food in absolute security. N. saw them at the Castle being packed with men; nineteen got in packed like herrings, and three remained outside. Up came the sergeant: "Now then, gentlemen, move up, move up: the car held twenty-two yesterday; it must hold twenty-two to-day"; and in the unfortunate three were stuffed. It must have been suffocating, but they were taken to their positions in absolute safety.

Saturday, 29th, 10 a.m.

Last night was an agitating one. The sniper was very active, and after dinner several shots struck the annexe, one or two coming through the windows, and one broke the glass roof of the bridge. Mr. B., who never loses his head, decided to get all the people out of the annexe, with staff (about forty people); and all we in the main building, whose rooms look out on the back, were forbidden to have lights in our rooms at all. There was such a strong feeling of uneasiness throughout the hotel, and always the danger of its being set on fire, that about 10 p.m. H. said we must be prepared at any moment to leave the hotel if necessary. So we went up to our room and in pitch darkness groped about and collected a few things (F.'s miniature and the presentation portrait of him, my despatch case with his letters, my fur coat, hat and boots), and we took them down to the sitting-room, which H. uses as an office, on the first floor. All the people in the hotel were collected in the lounge, which is very large and faces the street, and the whole of the back was in complete darkness. The firing quieted down, and about 11.30 we crept up to our room and lay down in our clothes. When dawn broke I got up and undressed and had two hours' sleep. All the rest of the guests spent the night in the lounge.

This morning we hear an officer has been to say that the shots fired into the hotel last night were fired by the military. People were constantly pulling up their blinds for a moment with the lights on to look at the city on fire, and the military have orders to fire on anything that resembles signalling without asking questions.

Reliable news has come in this morning that nothing remains of the G.P.O. but the four main walls and the great portico. It is absolutely burnt out. The fires last night were terrible, but we dared not look out. Eason's Library and all the shops and buildings between O'Connell Bridge and the G.P.O. on both sides of Sackville Street are gone.

It is difficult to think of the position without intense bitterness, though God knows it is the last thing one wishes for at such a time. In pandering to Sir E. Carson's fanaticism and allowing him to raise a body of 100,000 armed men for the sole purpose of rebellion and provisional government the Government tied their own hands and rendered it extremely difficult to stop the arming of another body of men, known to be disloyal, but whose *avowed* reason was the internal defence of Ireland! In Ulster the wind was sown, and, my God, we have reaped the whirlwind!

We hear that many of our wounded are being sent to Belfast, as the hospitals here are crowded, and the food problem must soon become acute. Mr. O'B. told me his ambulance picked up four wounded, three men and a woman, and took them to the nearest hospital. The woman was dying, so they stopped at a church and picked up a priest; arrived at the hospital the authorities said they could not possibly take them in as they had not enough food for those they had already taken, but when they saw the condition of the woman they took her in to die, and the others had to be taken elsewhere.

If the main walls of the G.P.O. remain standing it may be we shall find the safe in H.'s room still intact. It was built into the wall, and my jewel-case was in it, but all our silver, old engravings, and other valuables were stored in the great mahogany cupboards when we gave up our house in the autumn, as being the safest place in Dublin.

4 p.m.

Sir M. N. has just rung up to say the rebels have surrendered unconditionally. We have no details, and the firing continues in various parts of the town. But if the leaders have surrendered it can only be a question of a few hours before peace is restored, and we can go forth and look on the wreck and desolation of this great city.

So ends, we hope, this appalling chapter in the history of Ireland—days of horror and slaughter comparable only to the Indian Mutiny. This seems a suitable place, dear G., to end this letter, and I hope to start a happier one to-morrow.

Yours,

L. N.

Third Letter

Sunday, April 30th, 10 a.m.

Dearest G.,—When I closed my letter last night with the news that the rebel leaders had surrendered I hoped to start this new letter in a more cheerful strain; but while we were dining last night H. was rung up from the Castle to hear that the whole of Sackville Street north of the G.P.O. right up to the Rotunda was on fire and blazing so furiously that the fire brigade were powerless; nothing could go near such an inferno. There was nothing to be done but let the fire exhaust itself.

If this was true, it involved the loss of the Post Office Accountant's Office opposite the G.P.O., the Sackville Street Club, Gresham and Imperial Hotels, and other important buildings, and would have increased H.'s difficulties enormously, as it would have been necessary to build up the Post Office organisation again, with no records, registers, accounts, or documents of any kind—at best a stupendous task. However, fortunately this morning we hear the reports were exaggerated. The Imperial Hotel, Clery's great shop, and one or two others were burnt, but the upper part of the street escaped, and the Accountant's Office and the Sackville Street Club were not touched.

This morning Mr. C, who has been H.'s great support all through this trying time (his second in command being away ill), and several other members of the staff are coming here, and with H. they are going down to see what remains of the G.P.O. It is being guarded from looters, as, from the enormous number of telegraph instruments destroyed, there must be a large quantity of copper and other metal,—a very valuable asset,—and also several thousand pounds in cash for payment of staff and soldiers' dependants, besides heaps of other valuable property.

Here I must tell you how absolutely heroic the telephone staff have been at the Exchange. It is in a building a considerable distance from the G.P.O., and the Sinn Feiners have made great efforts to capture it. The girls have been surrounded by firing; shots have several times come into the switch-room, where the men took down the boards from the back of the switchboards and arranged them as shelters over the girls' heads to protect them from bullets and broken glass. Eight snipers have been shot on buildings commanding the Exchange, and one of the guard was killed yesterday; and these twenty girls have never failed. They have been on duty since Tuesday, sleeping when possible in a cellar and with indifferent food, and have cheerfully and devotedly stuck to their post, doing the work of forty. Only those on duty on the outbreak of the rebellion could remain; those in their homes could never get back, so with the aid of the men who take the night duty these girls have kept the whole service going. All telegrams have had to be sent by 'phone as far as the railway termini, and they have simply saved the situation. It has been magnificent!

The shooting is by no means over, as many of the Sinn Fein strongholds refuse to surrender. Jacob's biscuit factory is very strongly held, and when the rebels were called on to surrender they refused unless they were allowed to march out carrying their arms!

As the book passes through the press, I learn on the one unimpeachable authority that the story about Messrs. Jacob & Co., however picturesque, is purely apocryphal.

M.L.N.

THE SINN FEIN REBELLION AS I SAW IT, page 59.

It is said that when Jacob was told that the military might have to blow up the factory he replied: "They may blow it to blazes for all I care; I shall never make another biscuit in Ireland." I don't know if this is true, but it very well may be, for he has been one of the model employers in Dublin, and almost gave up the factory at the time of the Larkin strike, and only continued it for the sake of his people; and so it will be with the few great industries in the city. Dublin is ruined.

Yesterday I made a joyful discovery. When we came back from Italy in March, H. brought back from the office my large despatch-case in which I keep all F.'s letters. I did not remember what else was in it, so I investigated and found my necklet with jewelled cross and the pink topaz set (both of these being in large cases would not go in the jewel-case), also the large old paste buckle; so I am not absolutely destitute of jewellery. But, best of all, there were the three little handkerchiefs F. sent me from Armentières with my initial worked on them; for these I was grieving more than for anything, and when I found them the relief was so great I sat with them in my hand and cried.

This week has been a wonderful week for N. Never before has a boy of just seventeen had such an experience. Yesterday morning he was at the Automobile Club filling cans of petrol from casks for the Red Cross ambulance. He came in to lunch reeking of petrol. In the afternoon he went round with the Lord Mayor in an ambulance collecting food for forty starving refugees from the burnt-out district housed in the Mansion House, and after tea went out for wounded and brought in an old man of seventy-eight shot through the body. He was quite cheery over it, and asked N. if he thought he would recover. "Good Lord! yes; why not?" said N., and bucked the old man up!

Some of the staff who came here this morning had seen a copy of the *Daily Mail* yesterday, which devoted about six lines to the condition of things in Ireland and spoke of a Sinn Fein riot in which four soldiers and about six rebels had been killed. If that is all the English people are being told of a rebellion which 30,000 troops and many batteries of artillery are engaged in putting down, my letter will be rather a surprise to you; and as the news must come out, the English people will hardly be pleased at being kept in the dark. Such a rebellion cannot be suppressed like a Zeppelin raid. During the first three days our casualties were nearly 1,000; now we hear they are close on 2,000.[C]

[C] This was exaggerated, our total casualties being about 1,380.

The College of Surgeons in St. Stephen's Green is still held by the rebels, so the firing of machine-guns from the Shelbourne Hotel and the United Service Club goes on as before, and there is intermittent firing in all directions. I doubt if it will quite cease for some days, as these strongholds will not surrender. Also the incendiary fires will probably continue. The great fire in Sackville Street last night was no doubt the work of incendiaries, as all the fires had died down. There was no wind, no shells were being fired, and no reason for the outbreak, but with all the relations and sympathisers of the rebels at large the fires may very well continue.

The staff have just returned. They are quite unnerved by what they have seen; they report nothing left of the G.P.O. but the four outside walls and portico, so we have lost everything. They say it is like a burned city in France.

May 1st, 11 a.m.

I had no time to continue this yesterday, but during the afternoon three of the rebel strongholds surrendered—Jacob's, Boland's, and the College of Surgeons on St. Stephen's Green. From this last building 160 men surrendered and were marched down Grafton Street. It is said that among them was Countess Markievicz, dressed in a man's uniform. It is also said that the military made her take down the green republican flag flying over the building herself and replace it by a white one: when she surrendered she took off her bandolier and kissed it and her revolver before handing them to the officer. She has been one of the most dangerous of the leaders, and I hope will be treated with the same severity as the men. People who saw them marched down Grafton Street said they held themselves erect, and looked absolutely defiant!

To-day for the first time since Easter Monday the *Irish Times* issued a paper with news of the rebellion. Very pluckily they had brought out a paper on Tuesday, but it contained only the proclamation and no reference to the rebellion, but a long account of Gilbert and Sullivan's operas which were to have been performed this week.

To-day's paper bears the dates "Friday, Saturday, and Monday, April 28th, 29th, and May 1st"—an incident unique, I should think, in the history of the paper.

It contains the various proclamations in full, which I will cut out and send to you. Please keep them, as they will be of interest in the future.

The paper states that Sir R. Casement is a prisoner in the Tower. So he was not shot without trial, as we were told. It also gives a list of the large shops and business establishments that have been destroyed—a total of 146.

It really seemed delightful to hear the little paper boys calling their papers about the streets again, and they had a ready sale for their papers at three times their value. This so encouraged them that in the afternoon they were running about again calling "Stop press." Several people went out and bought papers, only to find they were the same papers they had paid 3*d.* for in the morning.

"But this is the same paper I bought this morning."

"Sure, and it is, ma'am, but there's been a power of these papers printed, and they're not going to print any more till they're all sold."

Another lady thought she would drive a lesson home, so she said: "But you said it was a 'Stop press,' and you knew it was not."

"It is, miss, but sure they hadn't time to print the 'stop press' on it!!"

("Stop press" is the latest news, usually printed on the back of the paper.)

Anyway, so great was the relief at seeing a paper again that no one grudged the urchins their little harvest.

Yesterday H. visited the Telephone Exchange, and a point was cleared up that has mystified everyone; and that is why, when the rebels on Easter Monday took every building of importance and every strategic position, did they overlook the Telephone Exchange? Had they taken it we should have been absolutely powerless, unable to send messages or telegrams for troops. The exchange is situated in Crown Alley, off Dame Street, and the superintendent told H. an extraordinary story. It seems when the rebels had

- 23 -

taken the G.P.O. they marched a detachment to take the exchange, when just as they were turning into Crown Alley an old woman rushed towards them with arms held up calling out, "Go back, boys, go back; the place is crammed with military"; and supposing it to be in the hands of our troops they turned back. This was at noon. At 5 p.m. our troops arrived and took it over.

This saved the whole situation. Whether the woman was on our side or whether she thought she had seen soldiers will never be known.

When at the Castle yesterday H. got a copy of *The Times* for Saturday, the first paper we have seen since Monday, so you can imagine how eagerly we scanned the news about Ireland. More has got out than we expected, but still nothing like the true position. We rubbed our eyes when we read that "two battalions" had been sent to Ireland, and wondered if it could possibly have been a printer's error for two divisions (40,000 men) which actually arrived on Wednesday. The people were in the streets of Kingstown for twenty hours watching the troops pass through. Since then many more troops and artillery have come in.

2 p.m.

I have just returned from walking round the G.P.O. and Sackville Street with H. and some of the officials. It passes all my powers of description, only one word describes it, "Desolation." If you look at pictures of Yprès or Louvain after the bombardment it will give you some idea of the scene.

We looked up through the windows of the G.P.O. and saw the safe that was in H.'s room still in the wall, and the door does not appear to have been opened or the safe touched, but the whole place has been such an inferno one would think the door must have been red-hot. Among all the *débris* the fire was still smouldering, and we could not penetrate inside. I picked up a great lump of molten metal, a fantastic shape with bits of glass embedded in it. It is bright like silver, but they tell me it is lead. It is quite curious. Do you realise, G., that out of all H.'s library he now does not possess a single book, except one volume of his Dante, and I not even a silver teaspoon!!

Everything belonging to F. has gone; as he gave his life in the war, so an act of war has robbed us of everything belonging to him—our most precious possession.

It has almost broken H. up; but he has no time to think, which is perhaps a good thing.

The old Morland and Smith mezzotints have also gone—things we can never replace.

Behind the G.P.O. was the Coliseum Theatre, now only a shell; and on the other side of the street was the office of the *Freeman's Journal*, with all the printing machinery lying among the *débris*, all twisted and distorted; but, worst of all, behind that was a great riding school, where all the horses were burnt to death.

If at all possible you ought to come over for Whitsuntide. You will see such a sight as you will never see in your life unless you go to Belgium.

When we came here H. was scandalised at the condition of the G.P.O. The whole frontage was given up to sorting offices, and the public office was in a side street, a miserable, dirty little place, that would have been a disgrace to a small country town.

H. found that plans had been drawn up and passed for the complete reconstruction of the interior, building in a portion of the courtyard an office for sorting purposes, leaving the frontage for the public office with entrance under the great portico.

So H. *hustled*, and the work was completed and opened to the public six weeks ago.

It was really beautiful. The roof was a large glass dome, with elaborate plaster work, beautiful white pillars, mosaic floor, counters all of red teak wood, and bright brass fittings everywhere—a public building of which any great city might be proud; and in six weeks all that is left is a smoking heap of ashes!

N. had an extraordinary find inside one of the rooms. About six yards from the main wall he found, covered with ashes and a beam lying across it, a motor cycle. It was lying on its side. He got it out and found it perfect, tyres uninjured and petrol in the tank, and he rode it to the hotel, and has now taken it to the Castle to hand over to the police.

May 2nd, 10 a.m.

Last evening after tea I walked all round the ruined district with N. and two ladies from the hotel. The streets were thronged with people, and threading their way among the crowd were all sorts of vehicles: carts carrying the bodies of dead horses that had been shot the first day and lain in the streets ever since; fire brigade ambulances, followed by Irish cars bringing priests and driven by fire brigade men. Then motors with Red Cross emblems carrying white-jacketed doctors would dart along, followed by a trail of Red Cross nurses on bicycles, in their print dresses and white overalls, their white cap-ends floating behind them, all speeding on their errand of mercy to the stricken city.

From time to time we came across on the unwashed pavement the large dark stain telling its own grim story, and in one place the blood had flowed along the pavement for some yards and down into the gutter; but enough of horrors. We came sadly back, and on the steps we met Mr. O'B. returning from a similar walk. He could hardly speak of it, and said he stood in Sackville Street and cried, and many other men did the same.

Last night after dinner we were sitting in the room H. uses as a temporary office overlooking the street, when firing began just outside. They were evidently firing at the offices of the Sinn Fein Volunteers at the bottom of the road. It was probably the last stand of the rebels, and the firing was very sharp and quick. We thought bullets must come into the hotel. I was reading aloud some bits out of the *Daily Mail,* and the men were smoking. They moved my chair back to the wall between the windows out of the line of fire; but the firing became so violent we decided it was foolhardy to remain, so we deserted the room, took our papers, and went and sat on the stairs till it was over.

Since then we have not heard a shot fired; and it would seem that as we were present at the first shots fired in Sackville Street on Easter Monday so we have been present at the last fired eight days later in Dawson Street.

Out of all the novel experiences of the last eight days two things strike me very forcibly. The first is that, under circumstances that might well have tried the nerves of the strongest, there has been no trace of fear or panic among the people in the hotel, either among the guests or staff. Anxiety for absent friends of whom no tidings could be heard, though living only in the next square, one both felt and heard; but of fear for their own personal safety I have seen not one trace, and the noise of battle after the first two days seemed to produce nothing but boredom. The other is a total absence of thankfulness at our own escape.

It may come; I don't know. Others may feel it; I don't. I don't pretend to understand it; but so it is. Life as it has been lived for the last two years in the midst of death seems to have blunted one's desire for it, and completely changed one's feelings towards the Hereafter.

Now, G., I will end this long letter, and my next will probably deal with normal if less interesting matters, but intense interest must remain in the reconstruction of this great city.

Surely it must be possible to find men who will rule with firmness and understanding this fine people—so kindly, so emotional, so clever, so easily guided, and so magnificent when wisely led. One prays they may be found, and found quickly, and that we may live to see a Dublin restored to its former stateliness with a Government worthy of the nation.

Ever yours,

L. N.

Fourth Letter

Thursday, May 4th.

Dearest G.,—I had not intended writing again so soon, but things are still happening that I think you will like to know, so I am going on with this series of letters, though I don't know when you will get them. But as by this time you will have seen N. you will have heard many details from him. How much he will have to tell his school-fellows when he returns to Shrewsbury to-morrow! I hoped to have sent my second and third letters by N., and in fact had actually packed them with his things. But when I told H. he said the rules were so stringent about letters that N. would certainly be questioned as to whether he was carrying any, and if he replied in the affirmative, which he certainly would have done, the letters would undoubtedly be confiscated and N. might get into serious trouble. So I had to unpack them again and must keep them till the censorship is removed, which will probably be in a few days. They have been written under much stress of circumstances, and are the only record we have of this most deeply interesting time, so I don't want to lose them altogether.

I am not too well, as they say here. The loss of eight nights' sleep seems to have robbed me of the power of sleeping for more than an hour or two at a stretch, and even that is attended often with horrid dreams and nightmares. But this is only the effect of over-strain, and no doubt will pass, though my head feels like a feather bed; so don't expect too much from these later letters.

Last night after dinner, when H. and I were sitting upstairs in attendance on the telephone, who should walk in but Dr. W. We had not met throughout the rebellion, so he had heaps to tell us. His wife and children were down at Greystones, and the poor thing had had a terribly anxious time, hearing nothing reliable of her husband or of her father, Lord S. What she did hear was that Dr. W. had been killed and also that H. had been shot in the G.P.O. She became so anxious that her faithful Scotch nurse was determined to get into Dublin and get news or die in the attempt. I must tell you her adventures, not only to show you how impossible it was to get into the city, but also it is such an extraordinary story of endurance and devotion that it ought to be recorded.

The girl started from Greystones at 2.30 p.m. on the Thursday, I think it was, carrying for the officers' home 14 lbs. of beef and 4 lbs. of butter, as Mrs. W. feared supplies would have run short, since nothing could be got in

Dublin except at exorbitant prices (7s. a dozen for eggs and 14s. for a pair of chickens); so the girl started carrying a dead weight of 18 lbs.

She walked to Bray (five miles) and took train to Kingstown; here she had to take to the road, as the line beyond Kingstown was wrecked. She walked to Merrion Gates along the tram line about four miles, when she was stopped by sentries. She retraced her steps as far as Merrion Avenue (one mile), went up Merrion Avenue, and tried the Stillorgan–Donnybrook route. Here she got as far as Leeson Street Bridge (six miles), when she was within 300 yards of her destination, Dr. W.'s house. Here again she was stopped by sentries and turned back. She walked back to Blackrock (seven miles), when she was again stopped by sentries. She then returned up Merrion Avenue and, seeing that all routes were impossible to Dublin, took the road to Killiney (five miles), where she arrived about 11.30 p.m., having done thirty miles. Here she got hospitality at a cottage and stayed the remainder of the night there, paying for her accommodation with the 4 lbs. of butter, but she stuck gamely to the beef.

Next day she walked five miles to Shankhill, when she met a cart going to Bray *via* Killiney, so she rode back to Killiney on it and from thence to Bray. She then walked the five miles from Bray back to Greystones, her starting point.

Arrived back, she reached home absolutely exhausted, having walked forty miles, and dropped down saying, "There's your beef, and I never got there or heard anything." Mrs. W. was greatly distressed at her having carried the meat back when so exhausted and asked her why she had not given it away. "And what for should I give it away when we'll be wanting it ourselves maybe?"

Next day Dr. W. managed to get a telephone message through to his wife and relieved her anxiety.

He told us that on the first or second night of the rebellion—he could not remember which—two ladies of the Vigilance Committee patrolling the streets at night came on a soldier lying wounded in an alley off Dawson Street, where he had crawled on being wounded. They went to Mercer's Hospital and gave information, and stretcher-bearers were sent out to bring in the man, the ladies accompanying them. When he was on the stretcher the two ladies walked up to the railings of St. Stephen's Green and gave the Sinn Feiners inside a regular dressing down, telling them they were skunks and cowards to shoot people down from behind bushes and asking them why they did not come out and fight in the open like men. Meanwhile the stretcher-bearers had taken the man to the hospital, where Dr. W. saw him.

"Well, my man; where are you hurt?"

"Divil a pellet, sorr, above the knee," laughing.

"Does it pain you?"

"Not at all, sorr. Wait till I show you." He pulled up his trousers and showed five bullet shots below the knee.

"What regiment?"

"Royal Irish, sorr, like Michael Cassidy, of Irish nationality; and I bear no ill-will to nobody."

Cheery soul! His great pride was that about forty shots had been fired at him and not one hit him above the knee.

Dr. W. must bear a charmed life. He told us of several escapes he had. One, the most dramatic, I must tell you.

You know he is one of the surgeons to Mercer's Hospital, and had to be perpetually operating there at all hours of the day and night, besides having his own private hospital, in which he takes wounded officers. It too was filled with rebellion victims, so his work was tremendous.

One night he left Mercer's about 1 a.m., accompanied by another doctor. When passing in front of the Shelbourne Hotel they were challenged by our troops there. On explaining who they were they were of course allowed to proceed, and they stepped briskly out, wanting to get home. Suddenly, on the same pavement, about twenty yards away as far as they could judge in the black darkness, out flashed two little lights from small electric lamps, evidently Sinn Fein signals. Dr. W. stopped and said to his companion: "Did you see that? it was a signal," when almost before the words were out of his mouth two rifles blazed straight at them, almost blinding them with the flash, and they *felt* the bullets whiz past their heads. The two Sinn Feiners, having signalled, waited long enough to see if their signal was returned, and then fired straight at where by their footsteps they supposed Dr. W. and his friend to be, and missed them by an inch or two.

Dr. W. and his friend got into the shelter of a doorway and flattened themselves out, trying to look as if they were not there, and quite forgetting that they both had lighted cigarettes, whose red tips should have been a beacon light to a vital spot had the Sinn Feiners noticed them. But for some reason they did not proceed further, and Dr. W. heard their steps dying away in the distance. Meanwhile his companion had his finger on the electric bell of the doorway where they were hiding, and after a time which seemed like an eternity an upper window opened and a voice inquired who was there, whereupon the woman of the house came down and let them in, and they spent the remainder of the night there.

Yesterday the Post Office was able to pay the separation allowances to the soldiers' wives. Last week of course it was impossible, but as it would have been equally impossible for them to have bought anything it did not so much matter. The question was how to get so large a sum of money round to the outlying post offices in safety, for, though the city is now comparatively safe, there are still snipers in outlying districts, and any party of Post Office officials known to have possession of large sums of money would undoubtedly have been attacked. So H. bethought him to requisition for one of the boiler armoured cars with military guard, and it was at once granted him. We had heard of them from N., but had not seen one, and great was the excitement at the hotel when this huge monster arrived for H.'s instructions. We all went out and examined it.

It was not one of Guinness's, but one that had been rigged up by one of the railway companies, with an engine boiler fixed on to a huge motor trolley, all painted light grey; and all down each side were black dots in an elegant design—something like this:—

Here and there one of these squares was cut out and acted as an air-hole, but they all looked exactly alike, so a sniper on a roof or from a window aiming at one of these squares probably found his bullet struck iron and bounded off to the accompaniment of derisive jeers from the "Tommies" inside.

ARMOURED CAR.

From the hotel the car proceeded to the Bank of Ireland, and took over £10,000 in *silver*, and started on its round to all the post offices, delivering the money in perfect safety. I will try and send you a photograph of one of these most ingenious conveyances.

After it had started on its round I went with H. to see the temporary sorting offices. H. had secured an enormous skating rink at the back of the Rotunda, and here all the sorting of letters was going on, with no apparatus whatever except what the men had contrived for themselves out of seats, benches and old scenery. They were all hard at work—a regular hive of bees. We think it is greatly to the credit of the Post Office staff that in twelve days from the *outbreak* of the rebellion and three days after the actual cessation of hostilities the whole service was reorganised, with two deliveries a day in Dublin, besides the ordinary country and mail deliveries. The engineers and telegraphists were no less wonderful. Indeed the staff from top to bottom of the office have worked splendidly, and H. is very proud of them. We looked in at the poor G.P.O. on our way back. It is still smouldering, and it will be quite a fortnight before any excavations can be begun, but H. hopes to get the safe that contains many of our treasures out of the wall and opened in a few days.

To-day a Dr. C. who is staying in the hotel told me of an extraordinary escape he had had during one of the days of the rebellion. He was walking through one of the squares, which he had been told was clear of snipers, with an old friend of about eighty, when suddenly a bullet struck the pavement at the feet of his friend and ricochetted off. It was within an inch of the old gentleman's feet, and he was greatly interested, wanting to find the bullet to keep as a memento. While they were looking about for it a man who had been walking just behind them passed them on the pavement, and had only gone a few yards when they heard a second rifle shot, and the man dropped like a stone, shot through the heart. Dr. C. ran up to him, but he was quite dead. There was absolutely no safety anywhere from the snipers; man, woman, or child, nothing came amiss to them. It was dastardly fighting, if it could be called fighting at all.

A few days after St. Stephen's Green was supposed to have been cleared of rebels, we were told of a young woman whose husband was home from the war wounded and in one of the hospitals. She was going to see him, so took a short cut through the Green, when she was shot through the thigh; it is supposed by a rebel, in hiding in the shrubberies.

Sunday, 7th.

I am sending off my other letters to you to-morrow, as we hear the censorship is no longer so strict, and as from the papers the position here seems now to be known in England private letters are not likely to be stopped. I will keep this till the safe is opened and tell you the result.

To-day Mr. O'B. brought his wife to see me, and they have offered us their lovely house, Celbridge Abbey, about ten miles from Dublin, for five or six weeks from June 1st as they are going abroad again, and they thought we should like it for a change. We are more than grateful, as all our plans for going to Greystones for June and July are knocked on the head; but to Celbridge there is a good train service, and H. can come into Dublin every day, while I can revel in the lovely garden and grounds and recover in the peace and quiet my lost powers of sleep. What a kind thought it is, and how welcome at such a time! Celbridge Abbey was the home of Swift's "Vanessa," and later of Grattan, Ireland's greatest orator, so is a most interesting and historical place.

17th.

To-day the safe was opened, and contained nothing of any value,—only a few official papers!

With this has gone our last hope of any salvage from the wreck of our property. Dillon's "perfect gentlemen," of whom he expressed himself so proud in the House the other night, had evidently broken open H.'s great official desk, and found the key of the safe and abstracted my jewel-case, F.'s field-glasses and several other of his much-prized possessions, and then locked the safe again. The only document they stole from among the official documents was F.'s commission. Why, we cannot imagine, unless the fact that it bore the King's signature made it worthy of special insult and desecration.

H. was very sad when he told me, but I think I am past caring about any possessions now. F. and all his precious things are gone. Nothing else seems worth considering. Perhaps some day we may pluck up heart to collect things again around us, but at present one can only feel, "Let the dead bury the dead."

20th.

To-day they are beginning on the excavations of H.'s room; the fire burnt with such ferocity that there is much less rubble in it than one would imagine. As you probably remember, H.'s room was on the first floor, with a storey above it. When the whole place fell in, H.'s room fell through into the room below, and a portion of that had fallen through to the cellars. The men are removing everything of the nature of bricks and iron and stone coping of the roof, and then four extra-careful men are to be put on to shovel up the rest of the *débris*, which is burnt to powder, and Noblett, H.'s confidential messenger, is going to be there to receive anything of ours that may be found.

Yesterday morning and this morning I have been down watching the excavations of H.'s room. It is quite like the excavations at Pompeii. Every shovelful is most carefully overlooked, and several of our things have turned up, though so far nothing of any intrinsic value. When I went there yesterday morning Noblett produced a great lump of molten glass of no shape or form with one or two metal nobs sticking up at odd angles. He thought it was the remains of a cruet, but we had none; and on further examination it flashed across my mind that it was the cut-glass bottles in the large rosewood and brass-bound dressing-case in which I had packed all my jewellery—family miniatures, four gold watches and chains, diamond pendant, etc. It had been stolen out of the safe, and evidently the looters had not been able to get it away. Noblett was thrilled, and the men redoubled their carefulness, hoping to find some of the jewellery. When I went down again in the afternoon Noblett produced three little brooches that F. had given me on various birthdays when a wee boy. He always went out with his own sixpence, and nearly always returned with a brooch, which I used to wear with great pride. One, a Swastika brooch, he gave me when he was at Margate after that terrible illness, and he used to go on the pier in his bath-chair. The blue enamel on it was intact in several places; the other two were intact in form, but charred and black, with the pins burnt off. But how glad I was to see them again! During the afternoon two or three more brooches turned up, but nothing of any value whatever. So we came to the conclusion the rebels had broken open the box and taken out everything of value and thrown away the rest. The few burnt bits of jewellery that were found all came from one spot.

This morning when I went Noblett had nearly a sackful of curiosities, which I sorted over. Evidently these were the whole contents of the canteen of plated things we used to take with us when we took a furnished house and put the silver in a bank, quantities of spoons and forks, black, and looking like old iron, many twisted into weird shapes, and the knives, which were new when we came here, without a scrap of ivory handle, and the blades burnt and twisted in the most extraordinary way. A most miserable-looking collection, fit only for the dust-heap.

25th.

They are nearing the end of the excavations, and nothing of any value has been found. This morning when I went I found them cutting into a mound of what looked like solid white chalk. I could not imagine what it could be, but the men told me it was the books that had been stored in one of the great mahogany presses; not a trace of burnt wood was found. I could not believe that books could be reduced to such a substance. I had expected to find quantities of charred black paper, with possibly some fragments of binding, and was quite incredulous. However, on examining it I found the substance was in layers like the leaves of a book, but when I picked some up it felt like silk between my fingers, and you could blow it away like thistle-down. Had I not seen it myself I should never have believed such a thing possible. Besides H.'s and P.'s books there were a number of great official books in leather bindings half an inch thick, but *all* was reduced to the same substance.

Noblett gave me to-day one of Princess Mary's gift boxes that had been sent to me by a soldier at the front; except for being black instead of bright brass, it was absolutely uninjured—the medallion in the centre, and the inscription, date, etc., perfect. The Christmas card inside and the Queen's letter were just black charred paper, but you could see the M. and the crown above it on the card. Also an antique brass snuff-box inlaid with mother-of-pearl turned up but little injured.

26th.

To-day the men finished their work on H.'s room. At the last about eight fragments of silver forks and two tablespoons were taken out and a foot of a silver sugar-bowl with a bit of something that looked like burnt tissue paper attached to it; and that was all that was found of all our silver. The half of a copper base of one of our beautiful Sheffield plate candelabra came out of one of the last shovelfuls,—and there was an end of all our property.

So that page is turned, and it seems a good place to end this over-long letter. On Thursday we go down to Celbridge, where with memories of Swift and the wretched and foolish Vanessa and in company with a beautiful swan and swaness, which bring their babies to the lawn to be admired and duly fed, I am going to rest and recuperate for the next five weeks and try to remember out of this awful time only the kindness and sympathy that has been shown to us by so many Irish friends. I shall not write any more of these diary letters unless there are further acute developments, which God forbid.

Ever yours,

L. N.

PROCLAMATION DECLARING MARTIAL LAW.

WHEREAS, in different parts of Ireland certain evilly disposed persons and associations, with the intent to subvert the Supremacy of the Crown in Ireland, have committed divers acts of violence, and have with deadly weapons attacked the Forces of the Crown, and have resisted by armed forces the lawful authority of His Majesty's Police and Military Forces:

And, WHEREAS, by reason thereof, several of His Majesty's liege subjects have been killed, and many others severely injured, and much damage to property has been caused:

And, WHEREAS, such armed resistance to His Majesty's authority still continues,

Now I, IVOR CHURCHILL BARON WIMBORNE, Lord Lieutenant General and General Governor of Ireland, by virtue of all the powers thereunto me enabling,

DO HEREBY PROCLAIM that, from and after the date of this Proclamation, and for the period of one month thereafter (unless otherwise ordered), that part of the United Kingdom called Ireland is under and subject to Martial Law.

AND I DO HEREBY call on all loyal and well-affected subjects of the Crown to aid in upholding and maintaining the peace of this Realm and the Supremacy and authority of the Crown, and to obey and conform to all Orders and Regulations of the Military Authority. And I warn all peaceable and law-abiding subjects in Ireland of the danger of frequenting, or being in, any place in or in the vicinity of which His Majesty's Forces are engaged in the suppression of disorder.

AND I DO DECLARE that all persons found carrying arms, without lawful authority, are liable to be dealt with by virtue of this Proclamation.

GIVEN AT DUBLIN

This 29th Day of April 1916.

(Signed) WIMBORNE.

GOD SAVE THE KING.

PROCLAMATION POSTED OUTSIDE THE GENERAL POST OFFICE.

POBLAGHT NA H EIREANN.

The Provisional Government
of the
IRISH REPUBLIC.
To the People of Ireland.

IRISHMEN AND IRISHWOMEN: In the name of God and of the dead generations from which she receives her old tradition of Nationhood, IRELAND, through us, summons her Children to her flag and strikes for her freedom.

Having organised and trained her manhood through her secret revolutionary organisation, the Irish Republican Brotherhood, and through her open military organisations, the Irish Volunteers and the Irish Citizen Army, having patiently perfected her discipline, having resolutely waited for the right moment to reveal itself, she now seizes that moment, and, supported by her exiled Children in America and by gallant Allies in Europe, but relying in the first on her own strength, she strikes in full confidence of victory.

WE DECLARE the right of the people of Ireland to the ownership of Ireland, and to the unfettered control of Irish destinies, to be sovereign and indefeasible. The long usurpation of that right by a foreign people and Government has not extinguished the right, nor can it ever be extinguished except by the destruction of the Irish people. In every generation the Irish people have asserted their right to national freedom and sovereignty; six times during the past three hundred years they have asserted it in arms. Standing on that fundamental right and again asserting it in arms in the face of the world, we hereby proclaim the Irish Republic as a Sovereign Independent State, and we pledge our lives and the lives of our comrades-in-arms to the cause of its freedom, of its welfare, and of its exaltation among the nations.

THE IRISH REPUBLIC is entitled to, and HEREBY CLAIMS, the allegiance of every Irishman and Irishwoman. The Republic guarantees religious and civil liberty, equal rights and equal opportunities to all its citizens, and declares its resolve to pursue the happiness and prosperity of the whole nation and of all its parts, cherishing all the children of the Nation equally, and oblivious of the differences carefully fostered by an

Alien Government, which have divided a minority from the majority in the past.

Until our arms have brought the opportune moment for the establishment of a permanent National Government, representative of the whole people of Ireland and elected by the suffrages of all her men and women, the Provisional Government hereby constituted, will administer the civil and military affairs of the Republic in trust for the people.

We place the cause of the Irish Republic under the protection of the Most High God, Whose blessing we invoke upon our arms, and we pray that no one who serves that cause will dishonour it by cowardice, inhumanity, or rapine. In this supreme hour the Irish Nation must, by its valour and discipline and by the readiness of its children to sacrifice themselves for the common good, prove itself worthy of the august destiny to which it is called.

Signed on behalf of the Provisional Government,

THOMAS CLARKE.
SEAN MACDIARMADA.
THOMAS MACDONAGH.
P. H. PEARSE.
EAMONN CEANNT.
JAMES CONNOLLY.
JOSEPH PLUNKETT.

MANIFESTO ISSUED FROM THE REBEL HEADQUARTERS, GENERAL POST OFFICE.

HEADQUARTERS ARMY OF THE IRISH REPUBLIC.

General Post Office, Dublin.

28th April 1916—9.30 a.m.

The Forces of the Irish Republic, which was proclaimed in Dublin on Easter Monday 24th April, have been in possession of the central part of the Capital since 12 noon on that day. Up to yesterday afternoon Headquarters was in touch with all the main outlying positions, and despite furious and almost continuous assaults by the British Forces all those positions were then still being held, and the Commandants in charge were confident of their ability to hold them for a long time.

During the course of yesterday afternoon and evening the enemy succeeded in cutting our communications with our other positions in the city, and Headquarters is to-day isolated.

The enemy has burnt down whole blocks of houses, apparently with the object of giving themselves a clear field for the play of artillery and field guns against us.

We have been bombarded during the evening and night by shrapnel and machine-gun fire, but without material damage to our position, which is of great strength.

We are busy completing arrangements for the final defence of Headquarters and are determined to hold it while the buildings last.

I desire now, lest I may not have an opportunity later, to pay homage to the gallantry of the soldiers of Irish Freedom who have during the past four days been writing with fire and steel the most glorious chapter in the later history of Ireland. Justice can never be done to their heroism, to their discipline, to their gay and unconquerable spirit in the midst of peril and death.

Let me, who have led them into this, speak in my own, and in my fellow Commanders' names, and in the name of Ireland present and to come, their praises, and ask those who come after them to remember them.

For four days they have fought and toiled, almost without cessation, almost without sleep; and in the intervals of fighting they have sung songs of the freedom of Ireland.

No man has complained, no man has asked "Why?" Each individual has spent himself, happy to pour out his strength for Ireland and for freedom. If they do not win this fight, they will at least have deserved to win it. But win it they will, although they may win it in death. Already they have won a great thing. They have redeemed Dublin from many shames, and made her name splendid among the names of cities.

If I were to mention names of individuals my list would be a long one. I will name only that of Commandant General James Connolly, commanding the Dublin division. He is wounded, but is still the guiding brain of our resistance.

If we accomplish no more than we have accomplished, I am satisfied. I am satisfied that we have saved Ireland's honour. I am satisfied that we should have accomplished more, that we should have accomplished the task of enthroning, as well as proclaiming the Irish Republic as a Sovereign State, had our arrangements for a simultaneous rising of the whole country, with a combined plan as sound as the Dublin plan has been proved to be, been allowed to go through on Easter Sunday. Of the fatal countermanding order which prevented those plans from being carried out, I shall not speak further. Both Eoin MacNeill and we have acted in the best interests of Ireland.

For my part, as to anything I have done in this, I am not afraid to face either the judgment of God, or the judgment of posterity.

(Signed) P. H. PEARSE,

Commandant General,

Commanding-in-Chief the Army of the Irish Republic and President of the Provisional Government.

The day following this proclamation the rebels surrendered unconditionally.